ADVANCE PRAISE

"You are never in doubt about Ole Bentzen's ability. Many years of experience as a business manager and director have left him with considerable expertise. With his strong human relation skills, Bentzen has developed a practical philosophy, not only with structured theories, but also with a clear understanding of humanity. Bentzen is able to communicate the message to his listener so intensely that you gain a greater degree of human understanding as well as deeper self-understanding. You leave a session with Bentzen invigorated and bursting with new energy."

Alice Anastassia Ravn, Optician, Profil Optik Denmark

"In 2012 I embarked upon a life transforming journey – after 12 years working as a Danish diplomat, I started my own company: Shanghai Jungle. Not only did I go from a safe and comfortable life to be an entrepreneur, but I did so in China. The challenges involved in starting a business in a highly challenging market were substantial – sometimes overwhelming – and I was ill prepared for them. But as if by a miracle, I came across Ole Bentzen and his Nine Squares model for sustained business success.

"Today my company is thriving. I've been through ups and downs – and expect many more to come. But I believe it's fair to say that if it hadn't been for Bentzen's Nine Squares coaching, I would not have reached this point today. What Bentzen teaches is to get the basics right. How in the middle of the storm and adversity you can actually focus on what is right – and how this focus can set you on a path for growth. This is no small feat. There is no shortage of 'self-help' and 'business advise' books that aim to do just that. But in my experience, few of them are actually useful when you are in the middle of the storm. *Nine Squares* provides crucial clarity and is wonderfully operational. I unequivocally recommend it."

Alexander Schultz, CEO, Shanghai Jungle

"The book provides an easily accessible approach to how eye-level management can be implemented and performed – successfully. The Nine Squares method gives an overview and a connection that is logical and coherent. It creates clarity and structure and, not least, overview. A clear and simple vision is important, and not just to create, but writing it on a stamp, as noted in the book, is a good method. Definitely worth focusing on this method!

"The test provides a score that everyone can agree with and indicates at the same time the potential of your business (if you dare to be honest in scoring correctly!). Overall, working with the Nine Squares will provide results for those who choose to follow the eye-catching method – it is understandable and, not least, simple. Start in the upper left corner and create your vision and goals, follow the other fields, and you are well on your way."

Ole Lemvigh, Senior Partner and CFO, Resources A/S

Published by
LID Publishing Limited
The Record Hall, Studio 204, 16-16a Baldwins Gardens, London EC1N 7RJ, UK
524 Broadway, 11th Floor, Suite 08-120, New York, NY 10012, US

info@lidpublishing.com
www.lidpublishing.com

A member of:

BPR
Business Publishers Roundtable

www.businesspublishersroundtable.com

Printed in the Czech Republic by Finidr
ISBN: 978-1-912555-20-8

Cover and page design: Caroline Li

OLE BENTZEN

NINE
SQUARES

HOW TO BE THE BEST AT WHAT YOU DO BY
CREATING CALMNESS AND A SENSE OF DIRECTION

LID

LONDON   NEW YORK   BOGOTA
MADRID   BARCELONA   BUENOS AIRES
MEXICO CITY   MONTERREY   SHANGHAI

CONTENTS

FOREWORD

Good, better or BEST leadership is valuable because it creates happy employees and, in addition, satisfied stakeholders, customers, patients or guests, who will have an experience that goes beyond money-making and impersonal spreadsheets.

This guidebook is directed at leaders who wish to invest in their people, as well as their customers, to create a presence with quality, communication and digital presence. It addresses the visions and passions needed in a leader and the keys to success: creating calmness; having a sense of direction; communicating clearly; and getting the right results. This combination contributes to the core message of this guidebook, The Nine Squares.

The Nine Squares philosophy is a unique combination of elements, which enables you to play and learn about adding value – and consequently get results while having fun on the way.

Good, better, the best.
How to succeed.
Why and how I can contribute.

THE NINE SQUARES PHILOSOPHY

This guidebook tells you something about how we as individuals can act in line with visions, values and growth, based on meaningful motivation. This opens the door to positive processes, which are natural when seen from a broader perspective.

In 1976, I was in China, where I learned about and was inspired by 'The Legend of The Magic Square', also known as the 'Lo Shu Square'. This dates back to 650 BC when a Chinese master read the patterns on the back of a turtle and saw a deeper pattern that was based on the natural balance of the universe. The pattern on the turtle's back was divided into three rows of three. The Lo Shu Square was based on this – a mathematical grid where the sum of numbers from each row, column or diagonal is the same: 15.

Legend has it that a tortoise called Lo Shu appeared from a river and saved a Chinese village from flooding. The tortoise's shield had nine squares, with between one and nine dots in each square. And no matter whether you added up the dots horizontally, vertically or diagonally, the result would always be 15.

This book forms a practical model, which you or your business can use as a tool to create calmness and a sense of direction that will get you the right results. By testing the Nine Squares, you will find out whether you or your business are in the correct context. No matter how you choose to put them together, they will paint a picture of your values.

Having appreciated this Chinese legend, I have since applied the philosophy of 'The Magic Square' to management, leadership and brand work that I have carried out over the last 40 years. It has provided me with a formula which leads to results that are characterized by the sense of direction for which we each aim. This philosophy complies with nature's system and at the same time it provides direction in relation to being in balance with oneself, as well as one's fellow human beings.

This formula can be used in order to create order in an unpredictable world. It helps us get overall values under control and be prepared to learn and perform – with pleasure. The principal idea behind the Nine Squares philosophy used here is based on the unique context – everything fitting into the nine squares on the back of a turtle's shell – which makes it possible to incorporate all of your skills into your business, concept and brand. If this is then combined with the values of presence of mind and general presence, then you will achieve constancy and orderliness.

THE TORTOISE IS EVER-PRESENT...

The elements of the squares presented in this Nine Squares model were developed throughout my career, and have been shaped independently of the original Chinese mythology.

A MAGICAL SQUARE

I have encountered the myth of the tortoise on a number of business trips to China. However, it was not until the model of the Nine Squares had found its present form that I could see the relationship.

The magical tortoise must have been at the back of my mind and has since surfaced. It has caught hold of me and has helped me realize and communicate the Nine Squares as a tool and as a dynamic set of rules of conduct.

This model may be able to assist managers and businesses in getting back on track, remaining on track or getting ahead as a unique and innovative business with well-defined targets, visions and brand. This will result in a unique environment, which will be appreciated internally as well as externally – leading to staying calm, maintaining a sense of direction and achieving results.

I hope that you will be as inspired as I have been by the guidelines developed in this book.

Ole Bentzen

VISION

COURAGE

ATTENTION

PRE-GAME

COMMUNICATION

RELATIONSHIPS

GAME PLAN

KNOWLEDGE

RESULTS

THE NINE

SQUARES

The only constant of life is time. However, one's perception of time changes and, consequently, it is important to create a sense of direction as well as to keep up with the times and live in the present. We have to be adaptable – without losing our sense of direction.

A TOTALITY - A CONTEXT

The Nine Squares provide a picture of the totality and gives a systematic overview. By combining the intentions of the Nine Squares, the Nine Squares will indicate a simple way in which to reach a given target. The Nine Squares form part of a process where the attempt is to go from good to better to best. When you combine the Nine Squares, you will obtain the overview and the motivation needed to be good at what you do by creating calmness and a sense of direction.

TRIAD

It is vital that you understand the three essential factors or rules of conduct needed to do this. These factors are as follows:

- Time
- Energy
- Being in financial control

TIME

Times are constantly changing, that is the only thing that we know for sure. When times change, customers and the staff change. In fact, everything is changing. Now is already in the past.

It is about being ahead of time. If you do not keep up with the times, you will not be able to maintain your sense of direction or achieve results.

It is essential to understand the past, to learn from the past, to be in the present and reach for the future. You must create the required space and calmness for this to happen.

Creating a lifetime match means matching a business' managerial and staff skillsets with a given situation at a given time.

ENERGY - SEIZE THE CHANGE

The next factor is about energy, which is the investment made in order to achieve success. Use your time wisely and prioritize in accordance with this pattern:

- Use your energy and focus on learning, again and again – achieving additional competences
- Use your energy and focus on development and inspiration
- Use your energy and focus on being in balance both physically and mentally by means of presence – one thing at a time. This is quality time

FINANCIAL CONTROL

Money talks, and being in financial control is a vital prerequisite for the correct use of energy.

Make sure that you are good at keeping your business' cash flow under control – this provides positive energy.

It may well be expensive to be over-smart – this will not be visible in your balance sheet, but in your quality of life.

- Control your cash flow
- Be in control of the speed of progress

A strong vision creates
CALMNESS

VISION

CREATE CALMNESS

Time to stop and think.

Time to prepare.

Time to play and exercise.

Write it down.

....

....

....

....

....

....

....

Jot down your vision, on a stamp, and be clear, concise and precise.

You or your business should be able to write your vision on a stamp, and if you lose track or feel discouraged you can take out your stamp again and remind yourself of your original, clearly written vision.

Your vision should be closest to your dreams. If your vision is in place you will learn to say no when you are about to make a decision which is not in keeping with your vision and which will make you, your staff and your customers uneasy.

STORYTELLING

WITH STAR VALUES

Your vision should be based on your own or your business' values. If you do not include your own values in your decisions, you will not have the right energy and passion for your work, your professionalism, your processes or your project. Without your values, it simply makes no sense.

No business will be good, better or the best without storytelling.

Is it demonstrable? Can it be printed on a mousepad?

A text of no more than 100 words, which can fit into nine lines of storytelling, means a speech, which can be used and re-used, clearly and concisely and which, just as with the stamp, provides a spark of inspiration and appreciation.

My positioning, my stamp, my values.

My experiences, my feelings.

In conclusion: Write down your three-star values – they assist you by providing you with a sense of direction to make the right decisions.

What's at stake here is making sense, making a difference, making our presence real and important through values.

Why not write your stories and values on your mobile phone, so you have them close at hand – it is quite simple.

Calmness is your star story.

GOOD, BETTER, THE BEST

Every time I begin mentoring a new business, I start by testing the scope for improvement and considering how we can possibly get better.

We start out by using the Nine Squares for a test, according to which score one is good, two is better and three is the best. This gives us a clear picture of the values in the Nine Squares, as well as what we need to work on and improve and in which areas we can set achievable targets.

The next step is for me to test the staff in teams, so I can see if there are any correlations. Now we can set targets for the business as well as the individual teams. This makes it simple to understand and to optimize to obtain the best value.

A REALISTIC TARGET

In the 1970s, when I worked for a Danish business called Irma, one of my first business trips was a purchasing trip to China. During my trip, I stumbled upon some useful garden gloves. A Chinese tradesman showed me the different types of gloves that he sold while we were sitting opposite each other at a square table.

Some were castor gloves, soft and comfortable, some had practical edging and storm cuffs and some would wear well and had reinforcements in the most exposed areas. I considered which ones to choose, but I was trying to achieve everything with just one type of glove. The tradesman looked at me calmly, took my business card and said:

"Mr Bentzen – why make it complicated when it's simple?"

The tradesman pointed to the most practical glove and said:

"You buy this, I deliver."

And so he did, for many years.

This meeting was both instructive and epoch-making – a wake-up call for me. We met at a square table, so the situation was in balance, we were at eye level and the tradesman made the target realistic.

THE CHINESE TRADESMAN MASTERED THE FOLLOWING:
- Setting a clear target
- Being honest about what he would be able to deliver
- Making himself respected by putting himself in the customer's place
- Making it simple to create calmness

Visions, values and targets are interlinked – the first of the Nine Squares.

Since my meeting with the tradesman, I have been very focused on this particular skill: namely, to make my targets completely clear and realistic.

I have seen many managers fail in this respect by being caught up in unrealistic budget targets – and being incapable of meeting your targets is pure poison. Everyone gets demotivated, and excuses and explanations are brought up – this results in a loss of energy and it creates uneasiness. Set some realistic targets, split them into inter-mediate targets and learn to succeed through the value of presence.

VISIONS AND TARGETS

Communicate with yourself, invest time and work – a simple and meaningful vision ought to ooze through your business and create a sense of direction.

FIND YOUR VISION:
- What is important to you and what do you dream about?
- Is your vision simple enough that it can fit onto a stamp?
- Be clear and realistic when you communicate your target

Set a target which
reflects your vision

PRE-GAME

PLAY AND ACT YOUR

WAY TO LEARNING

A couple of years ago, I was contacted by a small IT firm with a view to persuading me to sit on their board. I listened to their pitch, but suggested to them that I would teach them about the Nine Squares instead. They were energetic and keen, but their business lacked focus and direction.

We prepared a pre-game, which was essentially a dry-run designed to unearth breakthrough ideas by being innovative and applying creative inputs to any kind of problem at hand. It was also a space to develop good practice for good habits.

The pre-game was focused towards getting the two founders to communicate. One of them was good with technical matters, whereas the other one had better interpersonal skills – but they lacked a joint sense of direction.

During the pre-game, we managed to get their vision and their targets in place. Their roles were allocated, we trained them on how they should come across as people and made a game plan for how to do so. As a result, the business found its sense of direction and became successful.

PRE-GAME, PROCESS AND PROGRESSION

If you prepare through playing and learning, you must constantly attempt to meet your targets. This is how you obtain energy, order, the value of presence and management insights.

Practice it, understand it and carry it out. You do this by preparing your pre-game properly and by working with lots of ideas.

There is now actual room for ideas. How do I meet my target; what can be done? Who does what, and when?

Once your pre-game is in order, complete what you set out to do before you scale it up to full size, practice it again and try to locate a good, better, or the best performance in a calm manner.

Finally, you must prepare a game plan as to how you intend to accomplish your plan. You will meet your targets by training your-self in using these factors – ideas, pre-game, process, completion and planning.

TIME TO WIN - HOW?

I have seen many businesses start up without realistic targets and with a vague strategy and values for which they do not fight. They simply did not prepare themselves properly.

The formula is to have clear visions, values and targets. Subsequently, it is practise that makes perfect. The more you prepare for everything, the more focus you have on internal tasks and on building trust and respect together, the easier it will be to win.

WHY?

Now you can spend time, energy and money on making sure that everyone's committed to working towards the same targets. This leads to advantages for everyone.

Making room for playing and learning results in a unified team spirit and a joint culture.

One of the best things that I ever did was to start up my own school. This enabled me to train my own winners, with whom I could communicate and facilitate, think of new ideas on an equal footing and create presence. The lesson is that you need to get to know your staff through social and emotional anchoring.

All of this means that you will all work towards the same target – namely, to create a team which feels culturally connected.

Build up your presence through values.

PRESENCE REACHES INTO THE FUTURE

Mentoring is about passing on something. For instance, an experienced person who is teaching younger individuals about culture and professionalism will constantly speed up the pace of change and improve performance.

DIGITAL OPTIONS ALSO EXIST

How do we translate our knowledge into another language?

How do we turn it upside down, develop it and add to it together?

We all wish for the same things – namely, to be present and use our professionalism. Your everyday lives will be full of responsibilities and discipline if you are always present by means of an everyday plan with targets, which are measurable and lead to development and improvement.

I was CEO at Irma and Thiele, where I implemented an internal school where pre-games could be tried, tested and perfected. For many years, I built up good business cultures as a result of this process. These were cultures which were based on understanding, happiness and always had the clear purpose of being the best. We want to play and learn – in order to perform when it comes to change, in relation to each other as well as our customers, hand in hand. We were pleased to deliver added value.

Invest in your staff, as they constitute good business.

Even today, I often meet former staff and our chats always tend to be about our good workshops where we pushed it to extremes – we learned from each other and were inspired by numerous guest lecturers. We shared our presence and gained value at our workshops – we added value in style. This is the best possible investment of your management resources.

Your staff constitute the business and the brand. This concept results in presence in every way, including emotional as well as social connections.

A WINNING MODEL

If you wish to introduce a separate environment into your business in the form of your own school, it is vital that you organize yourselves in such a manner that two, three or more staff are chosen and turned into pre-game masters. These masters will be responsible for the process, the planning and the completion. New skills will be practiced again and again. Additional masters are brought in from the outside in order to provide inspiration for development.

GIVE TIME FOR PREPARATION

Take turns being a pre-game master, as this will result in a higher level of involvement and commitment for the simple reason that if you have to teach others about your profession, you will be entirely responsible for your behaviour and how you come across.

And it is a useful process to be able to teach others. It gives cause for immersion. Try to give a speech: it is not that easy. Practice your presentation skills, as this will provide you with presence and value, commitment and power.

TRAIN FOR PRE-GAME AS FOLLOWS:
- Provide an example as to how you prepare and train yourself
- Do you understand your vision and do you practice it with your colleagues?
- Create room for learning, so that it is possible for ideas to flow freely
- Create calmness

The shortest way to
the target is, in practice,
always the longest way

GAME PLAN

MAKE
- AND BE PREPARED

A PLAN
TO ADJUST IT

One year, in the run-up to the Christmas sales, I went to South Korea in order to purchase something for Irma's youngest customers. My target was to find cute teddy bears with twinkles in their eyes.

I found a supplier with the right teddy bear and we agreed a deal to purchase 50,000. As Christmas drew nearer and the teddy bears were received at the warehouse, they did not have twinkles in their eyes. They looked angry and frowning. Needless to say, nobody bought the angry teddy bears.

I learned my lesson and adjusted my game plan. Subsequently, I invested in some chalky white seals with big, black, shiny and smiley eyes – and they proved a success.

This time I stuck closely to my game plan and ensured that everything went according to plan in all the stages of the transaction.

PLAN AHEAD

If you do not pre-game and plan how to meet your targets, you are sure to fail. I always plan ahead and go over the concept of the business in question before I start a mentoring project.

In most cases, the planning is rather opaque: nobody really understands who is doing what, when or in which connection. The spreadsheet has taken managerial control and is dictating plans within plans, from morning to evening.

There is no unity or cohesion, and the value of presence is nonexistent, or without any connection to the managerial visions, tools and habits.

WHY - HOW - WHAT - WHO?
Being able to answer such questions provides understanding, responsibility and a sense of direction.

I experienced a failure with regards to the above-mentioned teddy bear plan, which resulted in 'the angry teddy bear'.

HOUSE RULES - MUST HAVES
Check whether everything has been accounted for in the planning and whether everything is included in the spreadsheet.

This is where you will find the managerial planning tools. Everything must be covered. Lay down some basic, clear and fair house rules.

THE SUGGESTED PLAN IS DIVIDED INTO NINE TOUCH POINTS:

1. Your business, concept and brand plan
2. An ABC of your customer and product selection plan
3. Your budget
4. Your investment plans
5. Your cash flow
6. Your organization charts
7. Your management plan and cultural development plans
8. Your plan regarding interested parties and your relationship plans
9. Control x control x control

GAME PLAN

Planning creates calmness in the moment, a sense of direction as regards your performance and financial results. However, such planning must be up-to-date and flexible.

PREPARE YOUR OWN GAME PLAN:
- Use a previous game plan as an example
- Who is responsible for what? And what is the target?
- Prepare a game plan which allows the introduction of new targets and evaluation

CREATE CALMNESS

Create a general overview by means of calmness.

Combine visions, values and targets.

Prepare yourself and make a plan.

Pre-game, play in your own school/academy, and search for added value qualities.

The guiding themes
are direction, knowledge,
passion, communication,
body language and
the value of presence

KNOWLEDGE

CULTIVATE YOUR

KNOWLEDGE

Some years ago, when I was the CEO of the Danish optical chain Thiele, I visited our flagship store in Copenhagen.

Much to my surprise I was told that 36 pairs of branded glasses had been stolen. The glasses were stolen despite being fitted with alarm tags. The tags had simply been torn apart and left on the floor.

This incident meant that I became passionate about inventing a tag that would make a noise if it was torn.

A SIMPLE IDEA

After the burglary, I went to work on this project. I ran into issues again and again, such as the glasses being too small and many others. Nevertheless, I kept researching and asked many people for advice during the process.

I listed a number of requirements. One of them was that the spectacles should maintain their appeal in the displays and when the customers tried them on they should still feel that it was a pleasure. So, no big blocks or alarm tags, which might disturb the shape or design.

Having gained more knowledge and after investing my own passion, I applied for a patent on one of my ideas. After many adjustments, I finally received a letter to say that my patent had been approved.

My passion and knowledge, combined with the assertion of my story, had resulted in success.

YOUR PASSION IS YOUR KNOWLEDGE

Passion is what you are enthusiastic about, what you cannot be without and something that you take with you everywhere. Professionalism is the honour of being better at something. Wrap this knowledge and passion into your storytelling and tell others about your passions. Never think that the story is finished. By showcasing your knowledge, your passion begins to shine through as storytelling – building benefits, qualities and relationships.

Set up a system – the first step is communication.

A method, a technique, must be carried out with passion and a sense of direction.

Remember the finishing touches and to set out your story as an assertion, a declaration.

This is what I learned at Irma:

Always be the best and tell the stories behind the goods.

And finally, you need a good informative label for everything.

KNOWLEDGE

The starting point of all communication is to actually have something to communicate – and that is knowledge. If you respect the professionalism or specialist knowledge of others, then you will earn respect, too.

CULTIVATE YOUR KNOWLEDGE:
- Do you know your products to the full? And how about your competitors' products?
- How do you gain knowledge? Who knows more than you and how do you get hold of that knowledge?
- Cultivate your knowledge and share it with your colleagues and customers

COMMUNICATION

COMMUNICATE
OF PURPOSE

WITH A SENSE
AND DIRECTION

The square in the middle is connected to all the other ones. Now we are in the spot that represents real life; the moment of truth. This represents the amalgamation of the process and the project.

This means being capable of communicating with presence, with networks, with dialogue and with meaning. Plus, understanding the essence of the fact that communication means:

- To understand, to express and to do what you say that you intend to do.
- To be able to answer the questions as to what, why, when and how.

The word 'with' in Danish – 'med' – carries a deeper meaning. It's a dialogue between people at the same level, or in other words a neutral space which is open for deeper and honest communication. This is the vital part brought alive by style, tone and the use of words in context.

A stress on the 'with' leads to life, presence, values, organization and dialogue.

"Without trust, communication and honesty in any relationship – there is nothing to build upon"

This is how to obtain presence and it is where quite small things may have huge significance.

Communication with a sense of direction.

HOW TO COMBINE LEADERSHIP AND COMMUNICATION

LEADERSHIP:
- Communication – the language or the signals we use to express our experiences
- Presence and values – these are what ties it all together
- Competencies – this is about opportunities, ability, and the talent or skills to create value and added value with pleasure

Leadership is about combining communication, presence, values and competencies as well as being able to read the future. Leadership comes into being where there is a requirement for a sense of community, team spirit and togetherness, where all the relationships are connected by visions, values and preparation. Presence and values are key.

Leadership and togetherness characterize all good relationships.

IF THERE IS PRESENCE, THE FOLLOWING ESSENTIAL CHARACTERISTICS WILL FOLLOW:
- To delegate with a strong vision
- To communicate – and do so directly
- To create authentic conversations in strong and concise sentences
- To create positive energy – by means of enthusiasm, an upbeat attitude and presence
- To remember the little things
- To make deals and adhere to them
- To be ethical and responsible

COMMUNICATION:

Communication depends on language. This language includes accentuation, linguistic characteristics and non-verbal communication, which all signal values. Consequently, it is important to understand that we communicate by means of such signals.

This is the key to understanding and constructing a dialogue, to achieving presence and building communication with presence, and leadership by means of visions, values, learning, plans, efficiency and relationships.

Combine all of this and the storytelling becomes clear. The process should be fun!

Communicate *with* (as opposed to communicating *to* someone).

Be open, ask questions, listen and create a story together. Being co-authors will result in presence.

ARE YOU COMMUNICATING?
- Do you listen to your surroundings?
- How do you tell your story?
- Communicate your story together with others
- Set the direction

Routine is not allowed

COURAGE

USE NON-VERBAL
THE BODY

COMMUNICATION:
TALKS

They are saying nothing, but nevertheless their audience is laughing loudly. On a summer's day in Tivoli Gardens (the amusement park in Copenhagen), I witnessed a performance at the Pantomime Theatre and I noticed the magic of non-verbal communication.

The graceful ballet dancers managed to tell a story and bring about smiles and joy by means of their facial expressions and gestures. This made me realize how important it is to master your non-verbal communication.

According to surveys, 72% of any and all communication is non-verbal, and you need practise to master it – plus develop the courage to use it.

Being in the present time – and to perform with presence – is the key to mastering your non-verbal communication. In addition, you need words and intonation, both online and face-to-face.

You must be brave enough to perform in respect of all the touch points. Think about how many times a day that you perform. Formally as well as informally. You are *on* all the time and you are being weighed and judged.

It requires practise to master a good performance and therefore, through many workshops, I have introduced the idea that the participants will have a video made and edited about themselves.

Please spend 30 seconds recording yourself on video.

What are you saying and what is your face saying? How are you perceived by others? Your look?

These are the moments of presence. This is the moment of truth with regards to the value of presence.

COURAGE

It is by means of the backstage situations that you make sure the surroundings and the staff radiate presence and that the business vision shines through.

BACKSTAGE PRACTISE:
- Provide an example of when you practise your performance
- What do you miss when you have to perform and new relationships have to be created?
- Practise your courage and your performance – and then do it again

A SENSE OF DIRECTION

Create a general overview by means of a sense of direction.

Combine knowledge and passion.

Communicate *with* – not *to*.

Perform in style – and listen.

ATTENTION

A SMALL-SCALE
– AND A DIGITAL

OVERVIEW
LIGHT BOARD

In the Danish optical chain Thiele, we lacked a rational and objective manner in which to record daily achievements, including sales, the number of eye tests, the way the day went in general, as well as a way in which to measure professionalism, presence and efficiency.

Together with a number of staff, I started considering ideas as to how we would be able to measure everything, give rewards and make improvements.

The group came up with a simple model whereby we would measure everyone's efforts by means of red or green, a traffic light system. This required an investment. We pre-gamed and put everything into a plan – in other words we created a daily, small-scale overview.

At the end of each day, we would insert green or red lights into a score card for that particular day. It had to be a simple system, so that the top-rated actions resulted in quality and added value.

I invested several millions in an IT system, and as a result our daily lives were better arranged. The measurements were carried out by means of lights and every time we reached our targets, the reward would be a little something along the lines of ice creams, sweets or something.

The red lights were referred to as 'auxiliary lights', so we were able to visualize where improvements were needed in order to turn them into green lights and results.

NINE SQUARES

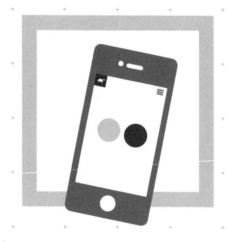

THE TARGET OF THE DAY

Green and red, a small-scale overview, was implemented into all the teams.

And every day we started over – we pre-gamed – as every day is a new day.

THE SMALL-SCALE OVERVIEW HIGHLIGHTED THE FOLLOWING:

- Today's target
- Today's professional efforts
- Who is doing what
- A checklist
- Personal pre-game
- Dress code
- Knowledge about the product ranges
- Knowledge about campaigns
- Control – control– control

Now we are ready for show time.

The customers are our focus.

Our professionalism and our smiles are in focus.

Even today I always introduce this idea, so that everything can be clearly seen in green and red lights.

Showtime and attention.

Now the moment has come and you only have a few seconds to create a connection, namely a connection between you and your guest, patient, customer, fellow citizen or colleague.

You are being judged – by yourself, too. Remember this every day. Every day is a new day. For a number of years, I have worked on how to release this energy at the right moment.

We prepared ourselves for being ready at the right time and we introduced a nine-second rule. This meant that we had a maximum of nine seconds from the time we met our customers until we were in contact with them by welcoming them with a smile and a hello.

This means being present with authority – to be helpful.

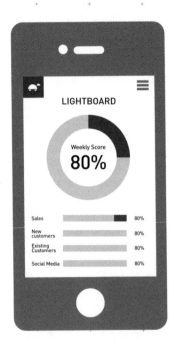

Lightboard – overview of green and red lights

ATTENTION

Attention is all about what shape you are in today: you have to be on and be confident. This is it, we are front-stage. Just like an actor, you have to be prepared, show presence and be ready.

SHOW ATTENTION:
- Do you pay attention to your customers and your surroundings?
- What do you do in order to be on the ball?

Follow your heart. Staff and customers go hand-in-hand and they will be in favour of your leadership.

Follow your heart. Staff and customers go hand-in-hand and they will be in favour of your leadership.

RELATIONSHIPS

RELATIONSHIPS
AND ADDED

WITH PRESENCE
VALUE

"That was one of your best speeches," my wife said after my nephew Benjamin's 30th birthday. I did not foresee any such praise when I was asked to give a speech on my way to the party. I considered what to say to my nephew and how to present his story.

I did my pre-game during dinner. I then called for silence and took to the stage. During my speech, I asked the guests what they thought the 'B' in Benjamin might stand for. One guest suggested 'well educated' (which begins with a B in Danish). I myself suggested 'compassionate' (which also begins with a B). When I asked them what the E might stand for, I was inundated with suggestions and we settled for 'energetic'.

The relationship had been created and the speech became compelling for both my nephew and all the guests.

STORYTELLING
- AND BEING EMOTIONAL

Once a customer, always a customer. You have to build your presence and your relationship on characteristics, advantages and benefits to the customers, so that the story about advantages, your business and your customer may contribute to an experience and a memory.

If this is the case, then you have created a relationship with presence and that provides results. It is a lifetime relationship. It is crucial that you are present and that you are giving us your attention right now. We all have a profound need for a sense of community and presence from within. We mirror ourselves in others, their needs and intensions. Our brains will automatically log on to this network and the sense of losing oneself in the flow.

Storytelling – and being emotional – constitute your building blocks when it comes to creating relationships. Successful moments provide lots of energy, happiness and commitment.

The sharing of experiences is a rational and an emotional experience. Sharing is a way to immerse yourselves in an experience. You have to make an active choice to be present, otherwise absent-mindedness and indifference will choose you instead. The key is to be active in a flow, focusing on presence. And make sure that you do not get caught up in unnecessary daily disruptions; instead, use your networks actively and have presence as a target.

Train your ability to be present, as it prevents many problems. The result is that you will build a relationship with lifetime customers.

SOCIAL INTERACTION
- PRESENCE COMBINED WITH VALUES

The system of red and green lights mentioned earlier provides an objective result. And if building relationships with presence is your target, you can set up your own club where you build on social interaction together through learning.

Presence means being fully aware and attentive in the moment. It means achieving insights by listening, letting things happen and being open without preconceived ideas or entrenched habits.

Presence means sharing a wider horizon regarding change.

The teamwork or interaction that shapes the situation is the means for continuous shared self-improvement through learning.

Presence means opening your heart and being able to see, learn and perform the totality as a prerequisite for creating or realizing future values. You have to be open and welcome future rational, emotional and social interactions.

The Nine Squares model provides coherence with regards to learning. It strengthens the facilitation of play and learning, and consequently the courage to be in the present with values, leading to added value.

The choice is yours. You will only know the results in the future.

RELATIONSHIPS

See the other person, show an interest and show that you care, and then you will create a story together as well as a relationship. It takes courage, sincerity and practise in communicating with the heart.

CREATE RELATIONSHIPS
- How do you get to know others?
- Give an example of when you last stopped and spent five minutes on small talk
- Take courage and share your story; be attentive

Added value,
togetherness, leadership,
a single overview

RESULTS

GOOD
– FROM BETTER

TO THE BEST

The results will start to show when you achieve well-earned trust and respect. Once your staff are flourishing you will know that you have respect and that you add value. So, this is your proof that by applying the individual Nine Squares of the model, you have achieved a totality – calmness, a sense of direction and results.

Added value with pleasure – the results will also be visible in your accounts.

This applies to any and all areas of business in that if you have a clear vision, realistic targets and continuous training, then you will remain at the leading edge.

The Nine Squares model provides the framework and is one way of achieving continuous improvement. By applying a systematic and holistic approach, we may train, play and develop ourselves and be in the present time and that provides calmness, a sense of direction and results.

RESULTS
Create a general overview.

Combine attention, rational targets and your relationship with emotional story building.

CREATE CALMNESS | A SENSE OF DIRECTION | RESULTS

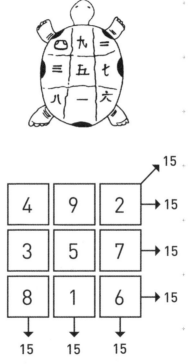

SCORECARD

This exercise is a quick way of asserting what you are best at and the scale of the potential the model can assist you in utilizing.

Consider what you are best at – write the number three in the relevant frame(s).

Feel free to mark several squares with the number three.

Consider what you are nearly as good at – write the number two in the relevant frame(s).

Feel free to mark several squares with the number two.

Write the number one in the remainder of the squares.

Add up the numbers to get your total score.

Total score: ....

VISION

COURAGE

ATTENTION

PRE-GAME

COMMUNICATION

RELATIONSHIPS

GAME PLAN

KNOWLEDGE

RESULTS

AN EXAMPLE:

The Nine Squares – the best possible score	27
My score	16

Scope for improvement	11

PRE-GAME TIME PROCESS:

Now it is time to invest in improving your scores in the individual squares, focusing on values and creating added value.

Stop for a moment and prepare.

VISION

COURAGE

ATTENTION

PRE-GAME

COMMUNICATION

RELATIONSHIPS

GAME PLAN

KNOWLEDGE

RESULTS

NINE PIECES OF ADVICE REGARDING PRESENCE AND VALUES

1. Presence and values are key. Take responsibility and face the reality
2. Pre-game in order to plan where you intend to gain added value. Set targets and start preparing
3. Pay full attention to your passion while you are present
4. Practise being in the present every day. Pre-game every day – the small-scale overview of 'what and who'?
5. Let any irrelevant thoughts go when you are 'on'
6. Perform well and listen with communication as your target
7. Energy and blood circulation – sleep is a basic requirement
8. Remember yourself and make time for spoiling yourself
9. An overview consisting of visions, values, targets and smiles

**NINE PIECES OF ADVICE REGARDING
YOUR MANAGEMENT STYLE**
1. Presence is your journey into the future
2. Know your strengths, time, place and competencies
3. Develop yourself continuously, together with your staff
4. Strengthen your competencies
5. Master the skill of communication
6. Become a digital star; use digital technology with presence
7. Stage and train everyone's sense of presence – build your own school of thought
8. Remember that leadership is built on being together, competencies, relationships, trust and respect – presence is key
9. Hurry up slowly and do not be too smart about it

YOUR WHOLE BUSINESS - YOUR BRAND
Write a little about yourself on the following pages.

Create and combine your own sense of calmness, direction and results.

YOUR NINE SQUARES SCORECARD

This exercise is a quick way to map out your strongest and weakest attributes within the Nine Squares universe. This gives you a clear overview of the areas you are best at and the areas where you could do better.

The most critical element in this exercise is being honest and truthful about yourself and your abilities.

For each square mark a score of 1 (good), 2 (better) or 3 (best). Then add them up to make your final score. The maximum score is 27.

For Example:
My score   16
Plus value   11
Plus value (%) 69

Now it's time to invest in improving the score in each field and focusing on the presence. Stop and prepare.

VISION

My score: ....

Room for improvement? ....

....

....

....

PRE-GAME

My score: ....

Room for improvement? ....

....

....

....

GAME PLAN

My score: ....

Room for improvement? ....

....

....

....

KNOWLEDGE

My score: ....

Room for improvement? ....

....

....

....

COMMUNICATING 'WITH' ('AND' NOT 'TO')

My score: ....

Room for improvement? ....

....

....

....

COURAGE

My score: ....

Room for improvement? ....

....

....

....

ATTENTION

My score: ....

Room for improvement? ....

....

....

....

RELATIONSHIPS

My score: ....

Room for improvement? ....

....

....

....

RESULTS

My score: ....

Room for improvement? ....

....

....

....

HURRY UP SLOWLY

Being in the present with leadership is your responsibility. In order to be part of the future, you will have to fight for freedom, which requires that you be good, better and the best when it comes to being present.

Freedom means that there is no limit to your passion. You will be able to do wonders because your passion is your friend. If you feel your passion, you can be anything and not just be tied up in whatever others have chosen for you.

Get to know your strengths, those of the others, your time and your place of refuge. There is a world to be won over, but aproach it with presence and leadership and it becomes your friend, so that you will take pleasure in creating something new.

Hurry up slowly
add value + yourself

Create calmness, a sense of direction, results.

It is better to be wise than wizened.

My vision is defined by my experience. I am wise and not wizened. I seek to share my knowledge – my experience, which I have collected over many years in the fields of retail business, design and franchise.

I wish to be active and to pass on my knowledge and experience, and consequently, I will not wizen, but will keep in form. When I give something of myself to the flowers, they will in turn give me back something beautiful. This is the way for both of us to ensure that we do not wizen; we shall stay in form and remain wise.

As a mentor, my added value is to pass on my experience, knowledge, best practises and comprehensive management style. The unique thing about the Nine Squares model is the idea of dividing everything into a crisscross pattern, which makes sense – good, better and the best.

CONTACT

The idea of the Nine Squares offers a tailor-made learning and development process during which you will be enabled to benefit from your own knowledge, train your presence and achieve your visions.

The starting point for the Nine Squares is each individual's own position and it consists of the following:

- Lectures
- Tailor-made training courses
- Personal coaching

Please contact us for further details as to how the Nine Squares may be able to assist you and your business with regards to calmness, a sense of direction and results.

☎ +45 6021 2537
🌐 www.theninesquares.com
✉ olebentzen@theninesquares.com

Yours faithfully,
Ole Bentzen

ABOUT THE AUTHOR

OLE BENTZEN has been an entrepreneur and author, as well as the influential Director and CEO for a number of well-known Danish companies, including the supermarket chain Irma A/S and Denmark's oldest chain of opticians, Thiele. He is known for developing a management model, the Nine Squares, that has inspired many young entrepreneurs today.

2014	Founder and CEO, The Nine Squares
1988	CEO, Thiele
1979	Non-Food Director, Irma
1973	Non-Food Purchase, Irma
1971	Export assistant, A. Michelsen Silversmiths A/S
1969–71	Niels Brock Business Academy
1967–69	The Royal Danish Guards
1964–67	Merchant in FMCG trading company

A MEMBER OF THE FOLLOWING BOARDS OF DIRECTORS:

2018	Light-Point A/S
2015	The Nine Squares Holding
2012–14	Niels Brock Elite, mentor
2005–06	Fields, chairman
1993–95	Danish Franchise, chairman
1992–95	Sahva A/S
1988–90	Deres A/S

NOTES: ....

....

....

....

....

....

....

....

....

....

....

NOTES: ....

....

....

....

....

....

....

....

....

....

....

NOTES: ....

....

....

....

....

....

....

....

....

....

....

NOTES: ....

....

....

....

....

....

....

....

....

....

....

NOTES: ....

....

....

....

....

....

....

....

....

....

THE NINE SQUARES HAS BEEN INSPIRED BY THE STORY OF THE MAGIC TURTLE LO SHU, WHICH HAS NINE SQUARES ON ITS BACK.

This book is directed at leaders who wish to invest in their people, as well as their customers, to create a presence with quality, communication and a distinctive digital identity. It addresses the visions and passions needed in a leader and the keys to success: creating calmness; having a sense of direction; communicating clearly; getting the right results. This combination contributes to the core message of this guidebook, The Nine Squares.

The Nine Squares philosophy is a unique combination of elements, which enables you to play and learn about adding value – and consequently get results while having fun on the way.